To all those who have encountered emotional hardship and who know, or will know, that the heart always emerges triumphant.

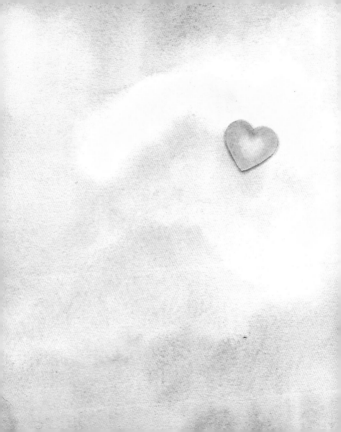

The Heart's Journey

By Judy Pelikan

Abbeville Press Publishers

New York ~ London ~ Paris

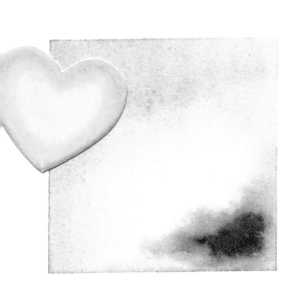

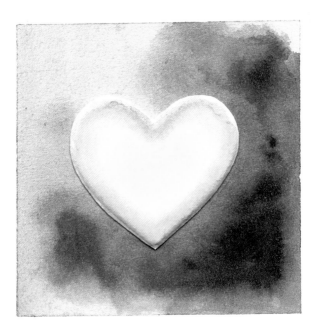

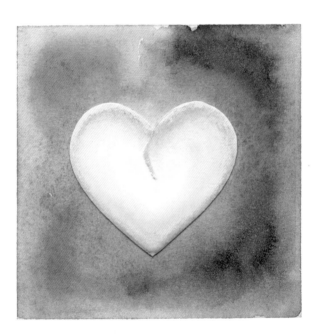

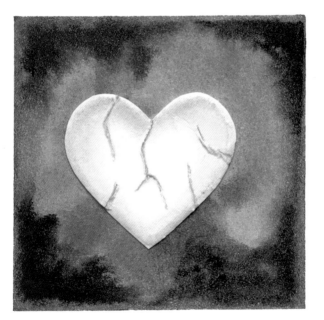

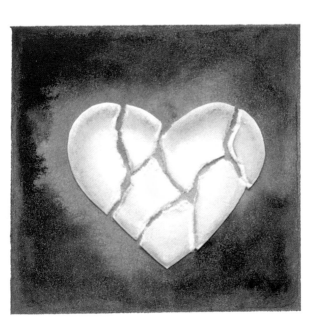

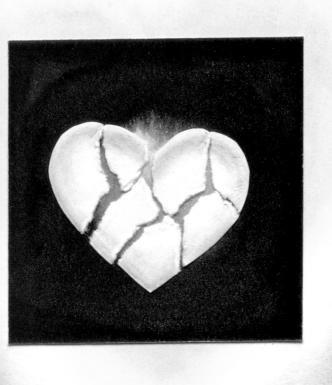

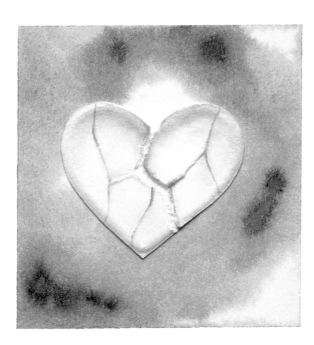

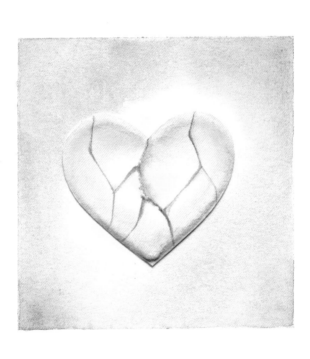

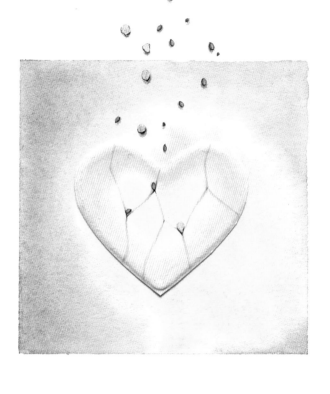

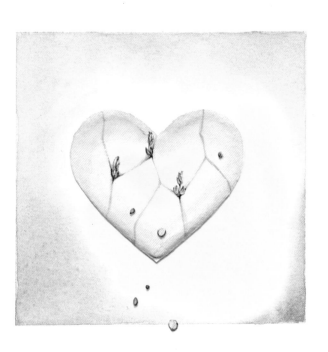

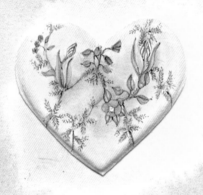